FROM THE PAGE TO THI

FROM THE PAGE
TO THE STAGE

Levi Tafari

Headland

First published 2006
by
HEADLAND PUBLICATIONS
38 York Avenue, West Kirby,
Wirral, Merseyside CH48 3JF

A full CIP record for this book is available
from the British Library

ISBN 1 902096 97 5

Printed in Great Britain by
L. Cocker Ltd,
Unit A9, Prospect St,
Liverpool L6 1AU

HEADLAND acknowledges the financial
assistance of Arts Council England

CONTENTS

FOREWORD

Like the finely-tuned movement of a dancer, athlete or musician, Levi Tafari's poetry moves effortlessly from page to performance, speaking directly to his audience. Levi dances with words and his words dance with him. This is physical poetry, poetry of sinew and muscle, rooted in the rhythms of the real world, but also poetry of tenderness, compassion and understanding.

Stephen Mitchell says in the foreword to his translation of Lao Tzu's *Tao Te Ching:* "A good athlete can enter a state of body-awareness in which the right stroke or the right movement happens by itself, effortlessly, without any interference of the conscious will... The game plays the game; the poem writes the poem; we can't tell the dancer from the dance."

Poetry is communication, communication between people, communication between minds and spirits. The writing on the page is an encoding of this communication, but it is the voice which lifts the words back into the air so that they can fly, carrying ideas from person to person to be received by the inner ear, to be embedded in the mind.

Levi's voice *is* the voice of his poetry - poetry which enlightens, educates and entertains. From the page to the stage, from community venues to concert halls, Levi Tafari has done it all. He has toured the world, both with musicians and as a one-man band. His recent visits to Jordan, Belgium, Ireland, Portugal, the Czech Republic and Germany, often working on behalf of the British Council, testify to his international reputation. His frequent appearances on television and his work with educators and community leaders demonstrate his ability to communicate the power of real communication.

As Levi himself says:

I planted a seed this morning
that will bring forth a tree,
a tree that stands like wisdom
with an inner creativity.

Dave Ward

1
THE
POETIC
STAGE

REACH FOR THE STARS

BOOKS ARE COOL
BOOKS ARE FUN   (CALL)
BOOKS SHOULD BE READ
BY EVERYONE   (RESPONSE)

BOOKS ARE COOL
BOOKS ARE FUN   (CALL)
BOOKS SHOULD BE READ
BY EVERYONE   (RESPONSE)

It's time to visit
your library
there you can borrow
BOOKS for free
BOOKS for the young
BOOKS for the old
in BOOKSHOPS
BOOKS are bought and sold

BOOKS on poetry
BOOKS about sports
BOOKS that are long
BOOKS that are short
BOOKS for girls
BOOKS for boys
with sound effects
that make lots of noise

BOOKS about ships
BOOKS on planes
BOOKS about cars
BOOKS on trains
BOOKS on animals
BOOKS on religion
BOOKS that give you
INSPIRATION!

BOOKS with Witches
casting spells
BOOKS that you can
scratch and smell
picture BOOKS
that have no words
BOOKS on insects
BOOKS about birds

Autobiographical BOOKS
portraying someone's life
fictional BOOKS
putting you on the edge of a knife
horror BOOKS
with a sting in the tale
BOOKS for people
who read in Braille

BOOKS on romance
BOOKS with passion
BOOKS on the famous
BOOKS on fashion
BOOKS on war and outer space
BOOKS about the people
of the human race

BOOKS that teach
you how to cook
you can even get
BOOKS about BOOKS
text BOOKS are used
in education
they are filled
with information

If you really want
to succeed
choose the right BOOK
and start to read
REACH FOR THE STARS
and you'll discover
now digest that BOOK
FROM COVER TO COVER

Because.....

BOOKS ARE COOL
BOOKS ARE FUN   (CALL)
BOOKS SHOULD BE READ
BY EVERYONE   (RESPONSE)

BOOKS ARE COOL
BOOKS ARE FUN   (CALL)
BOOKS SHOULD BE READ
BY EVERYONE   (RESPONSE)

I LOVE POETRY

I love poetry that's fresh and crisp
crowned with rhythm and rhyme
that inspires my spirit and touches my soul
speaking of what's happening in these times
poetry that's really kicking
that makes you move your feet
the type of poem you can hear
chanted out loudly on the streets

Jazzy poetry Bluesy poetry
Dub poetry and the notorious Rap
poetry that dances across the sea
and fills the cultural gap
I like poetry to tell me
how the poet feels
the type of verse that wakes you up
when the poet keeps it real

I love poetry that sticks in your head
designed to make you think
a poem that quenches your thirst
like a long cool tropical drink
a poem you can dance to
that liberates your behind
poetry that's challenging
constantly questioning mankind

I love poetry to be hot and spicy
that puts me in a good mood
when a poem hits the right spot
then I show my gratitude
a poem that's humorous
showing a little wit
that conjures up all sorts of images
now that's really poetic

I LOVE POETRY....

THE POET TREE

I planted a seed this morning
that will bring forth a tree
a tree that stands like wisdom
with an inner creativity

A tree not of the garden
but like nature it will glisten
you won't see it dancing with the breeze
but you will hear it if you listen

An array of ideas inspired this tree
plus the will to make it grow
planting seeds amidst the concrete
to breathe life into the ghetto

The trunk it bares the truth
words they form the roots
the branches along with the leaves
produce a pleasant fruit

Similes with synonyms
homophones and metaphors
come and see my tree flourish
with rhythm and rhyme at its core

Coloured with emotion
shaped with imagination
textured with alliteration
scented with information

Praising, Boasting, Rapping, Toasting
narrating on the way we live
thousands of years of tradition
to this tree life I will give

Images of antiquity
relating to modernity
rhythms of complexity
from my heart came forth this **POET TREE (POETRY).**

ALLOWED TO BE ALOUD

Some say poetry is boring
and should quietly stay on the page
but some of us make it exciting
as it rolls off our tongues on stage
Performing poetry to audiences
right across the seven seas
I'm sure if people lived in outer space
we'd be performing intergalactic poetry

I was browsing around a library
where some people were reading quietly
when all of a sudden a vibe took hold of me
I CHANTED POETRY SHOULD BE ALOUD

As I was wandering around a art gallery
I didn't hear a peep coming from anybody
it was if I was wandering around a monastery
I CHANTED POETRY SHOULD BE ALOUD

Sitting at the back of a quiet classroom
observing students revising that afternoon
I felt like I was sitting in a enormous tomb
I CHANTED POETRY SHOULD BE ALOUD

POETRY SHOULD BE ALOUD
LOUD ENOUGH FOR THE WORLD TO HEAR
POETRY SHOULD BE ALLOWED
ALLOWED TO BE PERFORMED ANYWHERE

I was at a theme park having wicked time
when the rides sent shivers up and down my spine
I nearly wet myself with a little urine
THEY SAID POETRY WAS NOT ALLOWED

Bubbling at a concert which was bombastic
the tunes they were dropping they were all classics
my honey and me were feeling romantic
THEY SAID POETRY WAS NOT ALLOWED

At the carnival festivities filled the air
out on the streets I was soaking up the atmosphere
the community was revelling it was event of the year
THEY SAID POETRY WAS NOT ALLOWED

POETRY SHOULD BE ALOUD
LOUD ENOUGH FOR THE WORLD TO HEAR
POETRY SHOULD BE ALLOWED
ALLOWED TO BE PERFORMED ANYWHERE

I just want the world to know
once you get into the poetic flow
you'll have difficulty letting go
THAT'S WHY POETRY SHOULD BE ALOUD

I just want the world to see
that poetry works therapeutically
in fact it's like performing tai chi
THAT'S WHY POETRY SHOULD BE ALLOWED

FROM THE PAGE TO THE STAGE

If this poem had the gift of life
what do you think it would do?
Would it kiss and caress
would it try to impress
by uttering the words I love you?

If this poem had the gift of life
what do you think it would say?
Would it be so profound
that you couldn't put it down
would its language blow you away?

FROM THE PAGE TO THE STAGE
THAT'S WHERE IT WOULD GO
FROM THE PAGE TO THE STAGE
WITH A NATURAL FLOW
FROM THE PAGE TO THE STAGE
MOTIVATING MANY NATIONS
THOUGHT PROVOKING
FEEDING INSPIRATION

If this poem had the gift of life
how do you think it would react?
Would it be so ferocious
that it became really atrocious
by putting you under attack?

if this poem had the gift of life
what do you think it would expect?
Would it expect the worst
then curse in every verse
would this poem have total disrespect?

FROM THE PAGE TO THE STAGE
THIS ONE GREW OUT ON THE STREETS
FROM THE PAGE TO THE STAGE
ACHIEVING EXTRAORDINARY FEATS
FROM THE PAGE TO THE STAGE
KEEPING POETRY ALIVE
FULFILLING ASPIRATIONS
STIMULATING VIBES

If this poem had the gift of life
what do you think its vision would be?
Would it start a revolution?
By fighting against pollution!
Would it lead us to true liberty?

Well this poem could have the gift of life
but it is entirely up to you
you need to chant it out aloud
in the midst of a crowd
you'll be amazed what life can do.

2
THE
EMOTIONAL
STAGE

THE FIRST WOMAN IN MY LIFE

A woman's work is never done
If you don't believe me ask my Mum
She worked her fingers to the bone
To provide us with a decent home
If she lived in Ancient Rome
She could have built that city on her own
She cooks, she cleans
She does everything
She irons decorates and does the shopping

She chastised us when we were rude
But never sent us to bed without food
Everyday she would change our clothes
If we had colds she would wipe our nose
Or if we went to Mum with a problem
Mum would always help us solve them
We didn't want for anything
We got the greatest gift Mum's loving
You can have ten aunties and scores of lovers
But remember you only have one mother
I remember when someone pointed the finger
Mum said I was Black, beautiful and I had a culture

She always made sure we went to school
Because in this life you can't be a fool
You see people will ride you like a mule
It was Mum who taught me to be cool
So mother there's something I want you to know
I love you Mum, I love you so
You taught me to survive in the ghetto
You can have my last **ROLO**

If it was not for you then I would not exist
So here it comes for you a kiss
Yes you was the first woman in my life
But one day I will take a wife
Then hopefully she'll become a mum
A woman's work is never done.

THE BLESSING IN MY WIFE

You are...
The icing on my cake
You are...
The cream of the crop
You are...
My sunshine in the morning
You are...
My love to the very last drop

You are...
The stars that shine so brightly
on a warm Caribbean night
You are...
The gracefulness of the hummingbird
You always fill me with delight.
You are...
The solution to my problems
Whenever push comes to shove
You are...
The beat that pulsates my heart
The rhythm of my love

You are...
The melody I yearn for
You are...
The lips I love to kiss
You are...
The butterflies in my stomach
You are...
My rainbow coloured bliss.

You are...
The Lily of my valley
You are...
My Rose of Sharon
You are...
My Queen Nefertiti
You are...
My Every Woman

You are...
The mother of our children
You are...
My one and only wife
You are...
Heaven sent from Jah Jah
You are...
The blessing in my life

TELLING EYES

My body fluids tingle
goose-pimples bubble and rise
this morning when your beauty
beheld my ebony eyes

The contour of your body
glowed with warm embrace
the silkiness of your skin
complements the detail in your face

You look so fresh
as the morning dew
another day is dawning
your natural beauty
shines on through
even first thing when my eyes are yawning.

I asked myself the question
How much beauty can one possess?
my mind explodes volcano like
and leaves me in a mess

The shivers that run down my spine
remind me I'm not dreaming
as passion gathers deep inside
my body chemistry is screaming

I drift for a moment into a world
where dreams sometimes come true
a world where eyes speak volumes
and mine say "It's great to wake up seeing you."

TALKING KISSES

Our tongues
brought us together
in more ways than one

Our first meeting
was "Hello, Goodbye"
the next thing you were gone

Sentences were exchanged
on the second occasion
then we wined and dined in public
at your place was the intimate celebration

Passionate kissing
game set and match
our tongues brought us together
two spirits attached

Now we have reached
that special bond
our tongues worked wonders
like a magician's wand

Every year we celebrate
from that moment on
the day our tongues brought us together
together to be as one.

DECIBELS OF JOY

I love it when you LAUGH
followed by your rainbow coloured smile
those decibels of joy
arouse the right places
the feeling drives me wild

I love it when you LAUGH
I'm so glad you made it mine
do it for me one more time
and send shivers down my spine

I love it when you LAUGH
for me it conquers fear
one on one or in a multitude
that *ire* sound I can recognise anywhere

I love it when you LAUGH
and I know I am the cause
don't ever take it away from me
I love it because it's uniquely yours.

nb: *ire* = good (Jamican)

BEAUTIFUL

Like SATURN
with her distinctive rings
you truly are unique
in your every style
features of beauty
so elegant and chic

You are always here
because you care
portraying a inner beauty
like queen Makeda
of Ethiopia
forever etched into history

You overstand my every need
we are seeds we grow together
soul mates who share
their every thoughts
closer to close
we are closer

So let me orchestrate
passionate words
to create a symphony
that arouses your ears
pulsates your heart
and soothes you spiritually

For the gleam in your eyes
when you smile
stimulates me like no other
an oil painting so radiant
I'm so glad you are my LOVER!

GOLDEN TONES

Through life we journey
not really knowing what life has in store
exploring life's avenues
hoping to learn a little more than before
a solitary spirit bonded
with a multitude of connections
touring the venues of expression
in one of many directions
igniting souls achieving goals
elevating to a higher plane
dropping the excess baggage
of restriction and pain
utterances of golden tones
spark and light up my ears
your voice materialises
but I know you're not here

I HEAR YOUR VOICE FROM A DISTANT SHORE
YOUR GOLDEN TONES MAKE ME FEEL SECURE
I WISH YOU COULD WALK THROUGH THAT DOOR
I NEED TO HEAR YOUR VOICE SOME MORE

My mission is set overseas
absence makes the heart grow fonder
in the stillness of the night
my thoughts for you they wander
the silence of space and time
architects such a gapping divide
the feeling to see and touch you
grows to have you by my side
the show must go on
I wish I could stay
but it won't be long
so let the music play

music is the food of love
for my daily bread I pray
that you will deliver your golden tones
to my ears without delay.

I HEAR YOUR VOICE FROM A DISTANT SHORE
YOUR GOLDEN TONES MAKE ME FEEL SECURE
I WISH YOU COULD WALK THROUGH THAT DOOR
I NEED TO HEAR YOUR VOICE SOME MORE

Dr Martin Luther King Junior had a dream
and now I have a dream too
some say we shouldn't dream
but that is not always true
my mission is accomplished
and I'm heading home to you
expressing this in some circles
is ridiculed or taboo
but I am a man with a mind of my own
I don't follow like a lost sheep
where there is sense there is feeling
I press the right digit so we can speak
it comforts me to hear your voice
when sitting here on my own
yesterday we used drums and smoke
today's signal is the telephone

I HEAR YOUR VOICE FROM A DISTANT SHORE
YOUR GOLDEN TONES MAKE ME FEEL SECURE
I WISH YOU COULD WALK THROUGH THAT DOOR
I NEED TO HEAR YOUR VOICE SOME MORE

OFCOURSEYOUCAN

OFCOURSEYOUCAN
OFCOURSEIWILL
OFCOURSEIDO

Are three magical islands
I would like to take you

OFCOURSEYOUCAN

Of course you can come with me
to this island of sheer desire
share intimate secrets mutually
igniting a passionate fire
we could explore for plenty more
but we have all that we require
just let love flow with clarity
like the beauty of a sapphire

OFCOURSEIWILL

Of course I will be your man
on this beautiful island of dreams
I will cherish you with all my heart
holding you in high esteem
on this amber isle of love and a smile
suggest a long life together
in the sanctuary of lush beauty
we will always love each other

OFCOURSEIDO

Of course I do is the sensual island
situated between the other two
of the three this island simply says
I will always love you
here a simple touch can say so much
as this island oozes with passion
the future glows love always flows
romance is our daily ration

So let me take you by the hand
as my feelings for you are true
let me hear the words OF COURSE YOU CAN
because you love me and I love you.

OUT OF THIS WORLD

You took me to the moon last night
in a journey filled with passion
we explored the wonders of the universe
in an erotic cosmic fashion

As we ventured into deepest space
discovering things anew
our surfaces moistened by the atmosphere
red hot erotic and blue

Drifting deeper into space
it's a feeling out of this world
we orbit each other's surfaces
as our journey unfurls

Our moans and groans are lost in space
as they become intertwined
we become oblivious to their sounds
another step for human kind

Now our mission is complete
as we climax at the summit
from the moment I held you in my arms
we entered another planet.

A MATCH MADE IN HEAVEN

When Father Time met Mother Earth
he gave her a great big juicy kiss
Mother Earth's temperature began to rise
now her life is filled with bliss

Father Time said to Mother Earth
"I will love you twenty-four hours a day"
to which Mother Earth replied "OOH! La La!"
then they began to play

Mother Earth then spun with joy
that made Father Time tick
they were destined to be together
their encounter did the trick

Now Mother Earth wrapped in Father Time
as he embraces her twenty four, seven
eternally they are joined together
a match made in heaven.

3
THE
NATURAL
STAGE

THE RICHES OF NATURE

A multitude of colours
display the riches of nature
creation forms images
developing an inviting picture
the sensation is one of beauty
bringing forth pleasure
as we awake we partake
contributing to enhance culture

ENERGY IS LIFE
LIFE IS FOR LIVING
BEAUTIFUL OUR MOTHER
EARTH KEEPS ON GIVING

The tree of life
sends forth its fruits of inspiration
go with the flow let life grow
a natural progression
we groove as we toil tilling the soil
in a positive direction
self expression through nature
the preservation of the nation.

TURNING THE WORLD INSIDE OUT

As I look out on the earth
I see land, sea and oceans
spirits roaming in and out
expressing their emotions
a variety of species on land and sea
preying on each other
the atmosphere so full of life
the climates of earth the mother

When new life arrived the spirits thrived
as they built a world through yearning
developments through Governments
that's when the fires started burning
so many died because some despised
when will they start learning
that ignorance is no way to advance
inside out the world is turning
inside out the world is turning

Anish Kapoor turned the world inside out
through experience and expression
manipulation of education
displaying his profession

This gigantic metallic donut sphere
distorts the reflections in the atmosphere
what's hidden its introverted centrosphere
a silver mirror forms its lithosphere

TURNING THE WORLD INSIDE OUT
IT'S ART IN FULL EFFECT
TURNING THE WORLD INSIDE OUT
HOW DO YOU CONNECT
TURNING THE WORLD INSIDE OUT
WHY NOT COME AND VIEW
TURNING THE WORLD INSIDE OUT
IS THIS THE WORLD FOR YOU?

THE REDUNDANT SUN

In the early morning of my years
I was told that the sky
was a magical shade of blue
so I scoped the classroom window
to find this was not true

The truth revealed
a contrary picture
of a boring shade of grey
the expression was bleak
in Britannia
the sky manifests itself this way

Rain and hail
danced down from the sky
the sun was absent
could it be the sun was shy?

The sun wasn't bashful
nor was it reluctant
the mood in Britannia
had made the sun redundant

Vacating Britannia for Jamaica
the sky revealed
a deep majestic blue
recollecting
what my teacher had said
her words now rang true

The sun played as it worked
with cotton wool clouds
animating life way up high
this painted for me
a whole new picture
of the matter we call the sky

The sun's radiance
shone its presence
for all who gathered there
the sun was working in Jamaica
and is now busy
twelve months of the year.

A GREAT PROVIDER

Trees provide a shelter
they feed us bearing fruit
producing cures through medicine
just boil and drink their roots

Trees we know have been around
from before antiquity
their long vertical distorted trunks
display a strange sight of beauty

Trees they stand so tall and proud
like a man decorated with honour
trees know what happened yesterday
and will live to tell the tale tomorrow

In forests and in jungles
you will find trees hanging out
trees they live in harmony
the tall, short, thin and the stout

Trees love the rain and cherish the sun
to supply us with the things we need
protecting us from diseases
cleansing the air we breathe

Now money does not grow on trees
it's time to realise
from trees we fashion instruments
so we can socialise

The wisdom of ancient Egypt
produced paper from trees
I really admire the Bonsai
nurtured by the Japanese

Now checkout this reality
a tree discovered gravity
centuries before Isaac Newton was a baby
a tree told me that when I was studying botany
Birds and monkeys dwell in trees
insects feast upon their leaves
around the world there are many varieties
trees the great unsung heroes of modernity.

THE WOOD TO THE WORD

FROM THE WOOD TO THE WOOD
THE WOOD TO THE WORD
A MAGICAL MYSTICAL
SOUND CAN BE HEARD

FROM THE WOOD TO THE WOOD
THE WOOD TO THE WORD
A MAGICAL MYSTICAL
SOUND CAN BE HEARD

Deep in the forest
a vibe can be found
we give thanks and praise
before we chop the tree down
to fashion a drum
that creates a beat
a wooden xylophone creates a tone
to make the music complete.

Animal skins vibrating naturally
wooden sticks rain down to create a melody
the music ventures to a new dimension
trees provide the instruments
for deep meditation
words exit the mouth
the tongues' communication
from the wood to the word
the power of expression.

FROM THE WOOD TO THE WOOD
THE WOOD TO THE WORD
A MAGICAL MYSTICAL
SOUND CAN BE HEARD

FROM THE WOOD TO THE WOOD
THE WOOD TO THE WORD
A MAGICAL MYSTICAL
SOUND CAN BE HEARD

The trees tell no lies
they can't disguise
the changes that are taking place
way up in the sky
Who'll take the blame
for the acid rain?
The rain that causes so much
pain in our eyes

Industrialisation monopolises
the earth turns to concrete
the environment dies
regeneration, conservation
find a solution
industrialisation
breeds destruction
take a trip on a train
to the absurd
from the wood to the wood
the wood to the word.

**FROM THE WOOD TO THE WOOD
THE WOOD TO THE WORD
A MAGICAL MYSTICAL
SOUND CAN BE HEARD**

**FROM THE WOOD TO THE WOOD
THE WOOD TO THE WORD
IF YOU LISTEN CAREFULLY
POETRY CAN BE HEARD.**

JAZZY STEEL

LISTEN TO THE RHYTHM
IT'S AS HARD AS STEEL
BRUSHIHG OUT A PATTERN
WITH A JAZZY FEEL

LET ME TAKE YOU TO A PLACE
WHERE THE VIBES ARE REAL
LET ME TAKE YOU TO THE PLACE
OF THE JAZZY STEEL

In the heat of the night
amber neon shines bright
on a smoked filled club
where the beat swings tight
an improvising horn
mimics the human voice
black and white piano keys
tinkle the freedom of choice
a deep double bass
strums a West African tune
silhouetted bodies dance
under the silvery moon
It's the Jazzy Steel
with a Be Bop swing
the drum beats the heart
when the lady sings
of a LOVE SUPREME
an astrological transition
vacating this world
on a cultural mission
the quest for the truth
takes on a new dimension
musicians explore the mysteries
of this complex creation

LISTEN TO THE RHYTHM
NOW TELL ME HOW YOU FEEL
LISTEN TO THE RHYTHM
IT'S THE JAZZY STEEL

Let Jazz take you to a place
where the men dress fine
the women look divine
the sweet scent of perfume and wine

Let Jazz take you to a place
where you can swing till you drop
doing the Lindy Hop
Jazz is the cream of the crop

Let Jazz take you to a place
with plenty of style
Yes! You can socialise
listening to DIZZY and MILES

Let Jazz take you to a place
where you can meditate
even demonstrate
how God is most great

Let Jazz take you to a place
where you can be free
to shape your destiny
no matter who you may be

Let Jazz take you to a place
way deep into space
a mysterious place
for a Jazzified race

**LISTEN TO THE RHYTHM
NOW TELL ME HOW YOU FEEL
LISTEN TO THE RHYTHM
IT'S THE JAZZY STEEL**

Jazz is free expression
with the added attraction
of improvising
while socialising

Jazz is that cultural stimulation
that inspires the nation
the temperature rising
Jazz is appetising

Jazz is satisfaction
an eclectic combination
of musicians revising
when the sounds are colliding

Jazz is a flash decision
cutting through the illusion
try recognising
Jazz is tantalising

It's the Jazzy Steel
with the hypnotic appeal
singing and swinging
the way you feel

It's the Jazzy Steel
revolving like a wheel
let Jazz take you to a place
where the deal is for real

**LISTEN TO THE RHYTHM
IT'S AS HARD AS STEEL
BRUSHIHG OUT A PATTERN
WITH A JAZZY FEEL**

**LET ME TAKE YOU TO A PLACE
WHERE THE VIBES ARE REAL
LET ME TAKE YOU TO THE PLACE
OF THE JAZZY STEEL**

STEEL APPEAL

Trains, planes, automobiles
all manufactured made from steel
bridges, towers, iron structures
steel's in effect I'm talking urban culture
heavy metal music as hard as steel
organised chaos with an aggressive feel
civilisation becomes a mechanised scene
and a micro-chip programmes the machine

With a number seven iron man makes his deal
turning the cogs of industry like a fortune wheel
so that society can shine with a metallic feel
you can shop till you drop that's the real appeal
then subliminal messages activate your brain
like an addiction consumerism gets in your vein
commodities wrapped up in attractive package
off loading junk on you like excess baggage

Now man makes move planning out his future
on the world wide web he's king consumer
yes surfing the net becomes second nature
but if all goes wrong he can blame his computer
now shopping at home becomes new ideal
a Big Brother scenario making life so surreal
man is losing his essence which is so unreal
as the quest goes on for a world of steel

We're now being driven nuts, bolts and screws
by the men of steel who have nothing to lose
protecting themselves with bombs, guns and knives
more metal devices this time designed to destroy lives
steel tanks make manoeuvres increasing our plight
it's a full metal jacket for the modern day knight
Eco warriors fighting against the metallic scene
trying to bring back the days when life was green.

PLASTIC FANTASTIC

PLASTIC, PLASTIC
IT'S FANTASTIC
MANMADE CHEMICALS
JUST LIKE MAGIC
ANY WAY YOU LIKE IT
THEY TAKE IT THEY MAKE IT
PLASTIC'S FANTASTIC
SO PLEASE DON'T BREAK IT

BAM, BAM, BAM (CALL)
DON'T BREAK IT (RESPONSE)
BAM, BAM, BAM (CALL)
DON'T BREAK IT (RESPONSE)

Anything you want can be made out of plastic
it's versatile it's really fantastic
laboratory tested it's scientific
I wrote this in an attic to make it poetic

Some plastics are soft some plastics are hard
people out shopping with their plastic cards
buying plastic plates and plastic spoons
vinyl records with plastic pop tunes
plastic combs and plastic phones
plastic bins to put more plastic in
leather trainers with plastic tags
sold to you in plastic bags
plastic stereos and video games
arty pictures in plastic frames
I went to the shops to buy some plastic shoes
There were so many styles which ones should I choose?

PLASTIC, PLASTIC
IT'S FANTASTIC
MANMADE CHEMICALS
JUST LIKE MAGIC
ANY WAY YOU LIKE IT
THEY TAKE IT THEY MAKE IT
PLASTIC'S FANTASTIC
SO PLEASE DON'T BREAK IT

BAM, BAM, BAM (CALL)
DON'T BREAK IT (RESPONSE)
BAM, BAM, BAM (CALL)
DON'T BREAK IT (RESPONSE)

A father gave his daughter a birthday gift
he was a plastic surgeon he gave her a facelift
he gave her a plastic nose
to match her plastic clothes
he gave her plastic BOOBS
from a silicone tube
her name was Cindy she had plastic skin
plastic all over down to her colouring
now she thought she was trendy
because she was bendy
but don't believe the hype
it was all plastic surgery

PLASTIC, PLASTIC
IT'S FANTASTIC
MANMADE CHEMICALS
JUST LIKE MAGIC
ANY WAY YOU LIKE IT
THEY TAKE IT THEY MAKE IT
PLASTIC'S FANTASTIC
SO PLEASE DON'T BREAK IT

BAM, BAM, BAM (CALL)
DON'T BREAK IT (RESPONSE)
BAM, BAM, BAM (CALL)
DON'T BREAK IT (RESPONSE)

Now big men acting like little boys
having lots of fun with their plastic toys
soldiers playing with their plastic guns
plastic bullets and their plastic bombs
the war on the streets is synthetic drugs
the police infiltrate with their plastic bugs
while the government acts all lardy-dardy
running this country like a Tupperware Party
their legislation tears the people apart

45

if stress creeps in get a plastic heart
people are not remote control, automatic
we're skin, flesh, blood and bones
we're not made of plastic

PLASTIC, PLASTIC
IT'S FANTASTIC
MANMADE CHEMICALS
JUST LIKE MAGIC
ANY WAY YOU LIKE IT
THEY TAKE IT THEY MAKE IT
PLASTIC'S FANTASTIC
SO PLEASE DON'T BREAK IT

BAM, BAM, BAM (CALL)
DON'T BREAK IT (RESPONSE)
BAM, BAM, BAM (CALL)
DON'T BREAK IT (RESPONSE)

DON'T BELIEVE THE HYPE!!!

4
THE
POLITICAL
STAGE

PARLIAMENTARY ERECTION

There is a trend that is growing in Westminster
it's cool and it's really hip
you see politicians are downing viagra
to maintain a stiff upper lip.

THE DISH OF THE DAY

**SATELLITE, SATELLITE
DISH OF THE DAY
SERVED TO YOU
IN THE AMERICAN WAY**

**AN ASSORTMENT OF CHANNELS
SATURATED IN LIES
SERVED TO YOU
LIKE BURGERS AND FRIES.**

In every city
all over town
the dish of the day
it can be found
transmitting images
through outer space
it's visual junk food
for the human race
A mind-watering feast
of television
an A la Carte menu
of communication
that whets your appetite
with a seductive flavour
it's entertainment
for the world to savour.

X rated channels
with busty babes
a coffee commercial
yes the couple gets laid
a fruity cough sweet
that seduces your neck
a whole banquet of programmes
sold through sex
Irate chat shows
that are hard to chew
public humiliation
for the world to view
bubble gum movies
to hype your imagination
frothy soap operas
that leave you with indigestion.

IT'S THE DISH OF THE DAY
IT'S THE DISH OF THE DAY
SERVED TO YOU
IN THE AMERICAN WAY.

A full table of sports
to suit every taste
magazine programmes
cooking at a racy pace
taste the many sounds
of the music scene
with the video served up
on your TV screens
Wild life, Documentaries
the News, Seller-vision
Cartoons, Sci-fi
Game shows, Religion
pleasing to the eye
when they're on display
on your satellite
the dish of the day.

You are what you consume
so be careful how you view
some say the contents of this dish
can have an adverse effect on you
distorting your mind
warping your very manner
it's as mal-nourished
as a TV dinner
so view, think and be merry
for tomorrow they'll try
to suck the very marrow
out of your mind's eye
for the programmes that they serve
on your satellite menu
might leave a bad taste in your mind
every time you view.

Because......

SATELLITE, SATELLITE
DISH OF THE DAY
SERVED TO YOU
IN THE AMERICAN WAY

AN ASSORTMENT OF CHANNELS
SATURATED IN LIES
SERVED TO YOU
LIKE BURGERS AND FRIES.

WHO'S BULLYING WHOM?

Sweat dripping
Lip tripping
He was very afraid

Pants wetting
He was fretting
He was gonna get paid

Tears falling
He was bawling
His life was cruel and grim

You see he was once a bully
But now a bigger badda bully
Is bullying him.

THE BULLY

He walks around
with a screwed up face
chest puffed up like a pigeon

His fists clenched tight
he's looking for a fight
he is on a mission

Abusive words
and nasty phrases
he intimidates his victim

He picks on people
who are smaller than him
that way he's sure to win

He controls a gang
they do his dirty work
this makes him feel important

When it comes to being nice
he says no dice
you'll find he is reluctant

Yesterday he went too far
hit a kid with an iron bar
and now he's in youth detention

The reason he bullies
other kids is he is
desperately seeking attention

THE GHETTO PART 1

TEN MISGUIDED GHETTOITES
fronting their props down on the frontline;
the drug situation
was getting out of hand
one O,D and ten Ghettoites became nine

NINE MISGUIDED GHETTOITES
skanking in the Blues to the latest Dub plate;
the police raided the Blues
someone had to loose
and now the Ghettoites they are eight

EIGHT MISGUIDED GHETTOITES
had a dream of living in Devon, Yes Devon!
the recession mashed up one's head
tearing their dreams to shreds
and now the Ghettoites are seven

SEVEN MISGUIDED GHETTOITES
became the victim of racist politics;
one was deported immediately
now the Ghettoites they are six

SIX MISGUIDED GHETTOITES
cruising in a car along "Rough Neck Drive";
now while they were Daddy Macking
there was a car jacking
and now six Ghettoites they are five

FIVE MISGUIDED GHETTOITES
fast living on the wrong side of the law;
a policeman bashed one
with a sophisticated baton
and now the Ghettoites they are four

FOUR MISGUIDED GHETTOITES
sat and planned a bank robbery;
they went deep undercover
one was caught on surveillance camera
four Ghettoites are now three

THREE MISGUIDED GHETTOITES
disrespect was all they knew;
so the community tracked one down
chased him out of town
now all that is left is two

TWO MISGUIDED GHETTOITES
waged war to see who should be the Don;
one pulled a gun
and the other tried to run
and now the Ghettoites are one

ONE MISGUIDED GHETTOITE
sussed out all his hommies had gone;
he couldn't survive
he committed suicide
and now the Ghettoites are none

This isn't make believe
it isn't a movie or a play
these incidents are happening in the Ghetto
each and every day
genocide in Hollywood might come across good
but it's time to change things
down in the Hood
Let the PEACE INCREASE
so we can live better
teach the youths to LOVE and RESPECT one another

IN THE GHETTO
IN THE GHETTO
IN THE GHETTO

WAKE UP FROM YOUR MISGUIDED WAYS.

THE GHETTO PART 2

ONE CONSCIOUS GHETTOITE
looked into himself and knew what he had to do;
he knew a mind was a terrible thing to waste
spread this knowledge and then there were two

TWO CONSCIOUS GHETTOITES
had a yearning for BLACK /AFRIKAN History;
their contribution
was second to none
so proud now these Ghettoites are three

THREE CONSCIOUS GHETTOITES
had a vision of what was in store;
to heal their situation
they formed an organisation
and now they have grown to four

FOUR CONSCIOUS GHETTOITES
through culture they learned to survive;
it was poetry, singing
music, painting and dancing -
culture has turned them to five

FIVE CONSCIOUS GHETTOITES
studied the science of genetics;
they appreciated their skin
was rich in melanin
now these conscious ones are six

SIX CONSCIOUS GHETTOITES
reasoned that ZION was their true heaven;
Ras Tafari chanting
Nyabingi drumming
spiritually now they have reached seven

SEVEN CONSCIOUS GHETTOITES
took control of their own fate;
to everyone's surprise
they kept their eyes on the prize
great role models now they are eight

EIGHT CONSCIOUS GHETTOITES
like stars they started to shine;
they shed their light
so clear and bright
their consciousness had now grown to nine

NINE CONSCIOUS GHETTOITES
grew into strong, respectful men;
in love with their female mates
they would procreate
and now these conscious ones are **TEN**

In these perilous times
we must regulate
LIBERATE OUR MINDS
to achieve that which is great

The ghetto is a metaphor
for incarceration
that is moving high speed
in the wrong direction

Where there is no vision
the people perish
if we stay unconscious
we are all bound to vanish

So wake up my people
there's no time to waste
it's time to get conscious
to improve the race.

IN THE GHETTO
IN THE GHETTO
IN THE GHETTO

NUFF RESPECT TO ALL CONSCIOUS GHETTOITES

IN THE HEAT OF THE NIGHT

On a long cold blue winter's night
Red-hot flames they were burning bright

FLAMES OF FRUSTRATION
FLAMES OF CONFUSION
FLAMES OF DISILLUSION
FLAMES OF REBELLION

Everyday people thinking things were all right
Until the peace exploded like dynamite

SPARKED BY EXCLUSION
FUELLED BY CONFUSION
IGNITED BY REJECTION
BURNING GHETTOISATION

IN THE HEAT OF THE NIGHT
IN THE HEAT OF THE NIGHT
THEY WERE BURNING THEIR PLIGHT
IN THE HEAT OF THE NIGHT

IN THE HEAT OF THE NIGHT
IN THE HEAT OF THE NIGHT
THEY WERE BURNING THEIR PLIGHT
IN THE HEAT OF THE NIGHT

Surrounded compounded
inna concrete plan
imprisoned for years
inna exclusion
Oppressed and suppressed
of their expression
ridiculed and tormented
because of their tradition

I see bloodshot eyes
filled with rage
I see youths on the streets
quickly come of age
I see the writing on the wall
appear from history's page
I see the invisible few
now taking centre stage

the media they came
the politicians did the same
seeking out the names
of those who lit the flames

Who will play the game?
Who will take the blame?
Who will stake a claim?
for the ones who lit the flames

IN THE HEAT OF THE NIGHT
IN THE HEAT OF THE NIGHT
WHEN THE PEACE EXPLODED
JUST LIKE DYNAMITE

GENOCIDE

GET FLAT OR GET SHOT
THAT'S THE SITUATION
MAN A LICK SHOT DOWN
INNA ENGLAND

GET FLAT OR GET SHOT
WHAT A SITUATION
GENOCIDE, GENOCIDE
DESTRUCTION

I used to feel safe I used to feel secure
I didn't have to think twice to step outside my front door
but life moves on everything must change
life on the streets is critical and strange
brothers on the corner waiting for deliverance
in their attitude and expressions I notice a difference
aggression seems to be the order of the day
step on a brother's toe and he'll blow you away

You see we are living in a vicious society
where guns on the streets are a reality
check the situation save the community
from these dreaded instruments of cruelty

I think for a while I ask the question
the guns in the ghetto where do they come from?
There are no gun stores in my vicinity
am I paranoid? No! it's a conspiracy
always the victims we are ghettoised
the system don't care as we act out genocide
Parliament cries out to arm the police
as if giving them arms will increase the peace

If you live by the sword do you know the prophecy?
A gun is an instrument of cruelty
arming the police will bring about a catastrophe
just study American society

Crack cocaine is bought and sold
a gun plays its part when you're taking control
of the profits to be made because luxury feels good
but these substances are destroying our neighbourhood
brothers treating brothers with disrespect
at the drop of a hat guns come into effect
two brothers had a fight a few seconds it lasted
one pulled a gun and the other got blasted

Black a kill Black situation slack
a brother inna pool of blood lying on his back
if you have to use a gun because you feel angry
learn to recognise who is the real enemy

**INNA BRIXTON, HANSWORTH AND MOSSIDE
GENOCIDE COMMITTING GENOCIDE**

**INNA CHAPLETOWN, ST PAULS AND TOXTETH ON MERSEYSIDE
GENOCIDE COMMITTING GENOCIDE**

As we watch the television we become anaesthetised
the gun is made romantic the way it is glorified
youngsters on the street with their water pistols
desperately imitating their screen role models
video games aimed at a teenager
on the screen it makes for practice on the streets it spells danger
on the school playground cops and robbers feel no pain
on the playgrounds of the streets another Brother is slain

He becomes another statistic on my TV
but this time it's for real it is not a movie
another family expresses bereavement and pain
we all show our condolences wondering when it will happen again

**INNA BRIXTON, HANSWORTH AND MOSSIDE
GENOCIDE COMMITTING GENOCIDE**

**INNA CHAPLETOWN, ST PAULS AND TOXTETH ON MERSEYSIDE
GENOCIDE COMMITTING GENOCIDE**

**GENOCIDE, GENOCIDE
DESTRUCTION**

**GENOCIDE, GENOCIDE
WHAT A SITUATION**

WAR

I saw them dropping bombs
firing sophisticated weapons
aggressing and oppressing
trying to destroy my nation
enforced occupation
they were taking control
vicious attacks
by devilish souls

They used military manoeuvres
and political strategies
yes displaying their might
causing a state of emergency
so we took to our ranks
to face our foes
who mutilated the land
filling our lives with woes

Land equals power
so the pressure must increase
power means control
so the sacrifice peace
sending reinforcements
in the shape of tanks and deadly planes
dropping chemical weapons
to inflict more pain

**WAR IS WAGED
IN THE NAME OF RELIGION
WAR IS WAGED
IN THE NAME OF RACE
WAR IS WAGED
TO CONTROL THE REGION
WAR IS DESTROYING
THE HUE-MAN RACE**

Like a festering wound
the earth's flesh starts to burst
the infection spreads quickly
as our plight gets worse
the smell of burning flesh
descends and pollutes the air
we see rivers of blood
and that's the price of warfare

**WAR IS WAGED
IN THE NAME OF RELIGION
WAR IS WAGED
IN THE NAME OF RACE
WAR IS WAGED
TO CONTROL THE REGION
WAR IS DESTROYING
THE HUE-MAN RACE**

**WE GOT TO STOP THIS HATE
WE GOT TO STOP THIS PAIN
WE GOT TO STOP THIS TERROR
AND REINSTATE PEACE ONCE AGAIN
WE GOT TO STOP THIS HATE
THAT CAUSES MEN TO WAGE WAR
SO WE CAN RETURN TO THE PEACEFUL LIFE
WE ONCE HAD BEFORE**

WAR IS DESTROYING THE NATIONS

GERM WARFARE

Bud was a stud
who drove the females wild
a good looking dude
with a seductive smile
out on the town
he was the main attraction
women came from out of town
to get a piece of Bud's action

Unfortunate one night
was the beautiful Lorraine
who loved Bud's style
life in the fast lane
the scene was set
for a heated night of passion
some serious sex
Whoops! Without any protection

Little did she know
he loved to spread himself around
he had a different woman
in almost every town
Lorraine bore the pain
as she became infected
like a leper of old
she was refused and rejected

It's difficult to know
what will happen next
you never think it will be dangerous
to engage in sex
now regretful of the day
she laid her eyes on Bud
as she slowly fades away
from his infected blood

GERM WARFARE COVERS THE EARTH
AND SOME DON'T HAVE LONG TO LIVE
THE SITUATION IS DREAD
NUFF PEOPLE AGUH DEAD
BECAUSE THEM H.I.V. POSITIVE

It is a world wide epidemic
of which yet there is no cure
it destroys the immune system
like a virus at war
which knows no prejudice
it knows no partiality
placing a death sentence
on this humanity

Some people show their fears
some discriminate
some demonstrate
by promoting hate
Yo! Check your lifestyle
because we're all at risk
life can be cruel
with a bitter twist

I watch a lot of speculation
when it all began
blaming gays I.V drug users
and Afrikans
non rubber users, drug abusers
this is not a gay disease
heterosexuals can be infected
so be careful please!

GERM WARFARE COVERS THE EARTH
AND SOME DON'T HAVE LONG TO LIVE
THE SITUATION IS DREAD
NUFF PEOPLE AGUH DEAD
BECAUSE THEM H.I.V. POSITIVE

The world has become
a dangerous place to live
you can get shot, struck down
or become H.I.V. positive
so look after yourself
take extra precaution
sex should be healthy
I'm taking rubber protection

Some people pray to God
seeking divine deliverance
others take a different route
of medical science
I contemplate
did A.I.D.S appear naturally?
Or was it an experiment
that went wrong in a laboratory

Many organisations
are now doing their best
to help the many victims
of a positive H.I.V. test
some wear a red ribbon
to show their support
do the right thing
so that you don't get caught

Because no matter what happens
we can't ignore
that prevention every time
is better than a cure
so stay protected
don't get infected
get educated
don't get infected.

Because....

GERM WARFARE COVERS THE EARTH
AND SOME DON'T HAVE LONG TO LIVE
THE SITUATION IS DREAD
NUFF PEOPLE AGUH DEAD
BECAUSE THEM H.I.V. POSITIVE

UNINVITED

Somebody raped my house last night
they entered without my permission
no they did not take away my dignity
but they stole many of my possessions

Somebody raped my house last night
penetration was made by force
the fact they were uninvited
provoked my anger of course

The person who raped my house last night
was thoughtless without a doubt
a power trip over the vulnerable
yes they struck while I was out

The person who raped my house last night
Was their action governed by need?
Were they destitute and homeless?
or was the motive plain old fashion greed?

Well I did not see this person's face
as they sadistically rearranged my place
by thrashing items around the room
it looked like a bomb had exploded BOOM!

Now the thing that got me real annoyed
items of sentimental value have been destroyed
plus my front door now needs to be repaired
I wish this assault had never occurred

I am now left to suffer the heartache and pain
my house has been violated will it ever be the same
and the psychological problems leading to strain
this crime could happen again and again.

STREETS OF HOPE

Stereotypes
media hypes
the victim Liverpool

They painted a picture
of a criminal culture
uncouth and very, very cruel

In vibrant times
poets created rhymes
and comedians carried the swing

There was MERSEYBEAT
the vibe out on the street
Yeah! Everybody wanted to sing

"You'll Never Walk Alone
In my Liverpool home"
L.F.C. wore the colours of success

They would beat teams up
while retaining the cup
teams who visited left distressed

Checkout the TV Soap
visit the Street of Hope
with two Cathedrals shrouded in fame

Newspapers from the gutter
distorted the disaster
Liverpool was back in the frame

I know people love the accent
but then some pass judgement
they say Scousers are always on the rob

"Well there is a Scouser in town
so screw everything down."
if you're a Scouser, it's hard work getting a job.

Some visit the Albert Docks
close to the Liver Clocks
and sail the Ferry across the Mersey

Checking out the famous skyline
which is recognised every time
with an image that is Oh! So chirpy

Well! She is known worldwide
this daughter of Merseyside
with a passion that burns like fire

So the reason I write
is to shed forth some light
and Liverpool you never fail to INSPIRE.

THE WORLD IN A GLASS

The world is a glass of Guinness
rich and very refreshing

The world is a glass of Guinness
nourishing and thirst quenching

The world is a glass of Guinness
tasty to the very last drop
where the black majority sits underneath
supporting the white minority on top

The world is a glass of Guinness
the nutrition is in the black
the white plays its part but only as froth
now what do you think about that?

The world is a glass of Guinness
take a look and see.

SPIRIT DANCER

A SPIRIT DANCER
A MUSIC MAKER
A DREADLOCK RASTA
FROM JAMAICA

YES! A MAN OF GREAT VISION
WHO GAVE I AND I A REDEMPTION SONG

A SPIRIT DANCER
A MUSIC MAKER
A DREADLOCK RASTA
FROM JAMAICA

YES! A MAN OF GREAT VISION
WHO GAVE I AND I A REDEMPTION SONG

Born in the district of Nine Miles
the music he created made Jamaicans smile
it spread across the world for us all to hear
it was A Natural Mystic flowing through the air
there was The Trench Town Rock, No Woman No Cry
the roots he proclaimed was Jah Ras Tafari
he didn't leave the children waiting in vain
hit we with music feel no pain.

A SPIRIT DANCER
A MUSIC MAKER
A DREADLOCK RASTA
FROM JAMAICA

YES! A MAN OF GREAT VISION
WHO GAVE I AND I A REDEMPTION SONG

A SPIRIT DANCER
A MUSIC MAKER
A DREADLOCK RASTA
FROM JAMAICA

YES! A MAN OF GREAT VISION
WHO GAVE I AND I A REDEMPTION SONG

Plant a seed sheriff wouldn't let it grow
that's why he shot the sheriff down in the ghetto
concrete Jungle no sun won't shine
Burnin and Lootin on the front line

but the Rastaman Vibration is positive
remember Garvey told us Wake up and Live
many had their doubts Bob taught us that live
come as a humble/Mighty lion thanks and praise to give.

A SPIRIT DANCER
A MUSIC MAKER
A DREADLOCK RASTA
FROM JAMAICA

YES! A MAN OF GREAT VISION
WHO GAVE I AND I A REDEMPTION SONG

A SPIRIT DANCER
A MUSIC MAKER
A DREADLOCK RASTA
FROM JAMAICA

YES! A MAN OF GREAT VISION
WHO GAVE I AND I A REDEMPTION SONG

Listen carefully the message will grow
many deep meanings from a few words flow
each is written for the world to know
the beginning of wisdom is to bend down low
light like a feather heavy as lead
down a Cain River he washed his dread
rock was the pillow to rest his head
on the cold ground he made his bed
reality, reality we just can't drift
easy Skanking meditate with a spliff
the healing of the nations he hailed this gift
the whole wide world he aspired to up lift.

A SPIRIT DANCER
A MUSIC MAKER
A DREADLOCK RASTA
FROM JAMAICA

YES! WAS A MAN OF GREAT VISION
WHO GAVE I AND I A REDEMPTION SONG

A SPIRIT DANCER
A MUSIC MAKER
A DREADLOCK RASTA
FROM JAMAICA

YES! A MAN OF GREAT VISION
WHO GAVE I AND I A REDEMPTION SONG

Coming in from the cold time will tell
who a reach Zion who a catch Hell?
Zion Train come take him away
the legacy he left us so much things to say
he said get up stand up stand up for your rights
chase those crazy ballheads and don't give up the fight
Because it takes a revolution to deliver a solution
find Jah in revelations it's the roots of redemption
Bob didn't worry about a thing
as he was jamming in the name of the Lord
through the movement of Jah people
Bob Marley songs of freedom always hit the right chord

A SPIRIT DANCER
A MUSIC MAKER
A DREADLOCK RASTA
FROM JAMAICA

YES! A MAN OF GREAT VISION
WHO GAVE I AND I A REDEMPTION SONG

A SPIRIT DANCER
A MUSIC MAKER
A DREADLOCK RASTA
FROM JAMAICA

YES! A MAN OF GREAT VISION
WHO GAVE I AND I A REDEMPTION SONG

NURSERY CRIMES

TRICKERY, TRICKERY DOCK
LIFE CAN BE A SHOCK
IN SPACE AND TIME
I CREATE A RHYME
THIS IS WHAT WE'VE GOT

There was a young woman
who lived in a shoe
she was homeless with children
what else could she do?
she marched on Downing Street
with ten thousand women and men
to evict those vampires at number ten

GET UP! STAND UP!
STAND UP FOR YOUR RIGHTS!
DON'T GIVE UP THE FIGHT!

Mean while…

Humpty Grumpty was doing so well
until a gunman shot him and Humpty fell
gang warfare what a dread situation
protection rackets and extortion
wheeling and dealing in illegal props
gangsters terrorise pursued by cops
paralysed from the neck down in a wheelchair
the community celebrates as he had them living in fear

And still….

John and Jane cruised down the Lane
to score themselves some crack cocaine
on their way there they got a scare
a police helicopter scoped them from the air
so they took two E's and went to a rave
now they're pushing up daisies from their grave

Now checkout….

Old Mother Hubbard
hid drink in her cupboard
she was always liquored to the bone

referred to a clinic
as an alcoholic
a celebrity her face was well known
along with media success
came adversity and stress
her career was trickling down the drain
seduced by the drink
drove her to the brink
a recluse she was never seen again

Just like....

Little Jo Weep
didn't loose her sheep
she hid them and claimed compensation
but the sheep were found
in her brother's compound
now the two are facing prosecution -
they could even go to prison

Ask yourself if this is a crime????

Georgie Georgie why oh! Why
did you kiss the girl and make her cry?
Georgie Georgie didn't have a reply
Well try man! Georgie, try man! Try!
So Georgie Georgie thought for a while
Then he turned to me with a sinister smile
he told me whilst he was making love to Emma
he accidentally called her Gemma
Gemma turn out to be her sister
now all three are starring on Jerry Springer

Just as....

Mary had a little lamb
which freaked the mid-wife out
genetic engineering Mary?

Yes! Without a doubt
laboratories in modernity
is this futuristic maternity?
This monstrosity appeared on my television
he was sporting a suit he's a politician
like an android he operates without a soul
this is the one who will take control

Finally....

Hey diddle, diddle
some are caught in the middle
trying to figure life out
talk of a god in the sky
watching from way up high
and to him we should be devout
stand and face your judgement
if you're disobedient
damnation dwelling in hell
but as far as I can see
society has placed hell around me
and they wonder why I rebel!
Yes they wonder why we rebel!

**TRICKERY, TRICKERY, DOCK
ARE YOU RECOVERING FROM THE SHOCK?**